The Corona-virus Prophecies

Were the Corona-virus pandemics predicted in the Bible? Have the causes and prevention been spelled out? Is there advice in the Bible for us to keep our cities and families safe?

By Pieter C Voges

Disclaimer

© 2023, Author P. Voges

Contents

1 Corona-virus prophecies

Does the Bible accurately describe the pandemics that we face right now? Let's start with the Exodus.

In the Old Testament, God called out His nation, Israel, out of slavery in Egypt. By miracle after miracle, they started their Exodus to the Promised Land. Egypt was cursed by plagues, diseases, and epidemics, but Israel was spared.

"And Jehovah said to Moses, Go in to Pharaoh and tell him, Thus says Jehovah, the God of the Hebrews: Let My people go so that they may serve Me. For if you refuse to let them go, and will hold them still, behold, the hand of Jehovah is upon your cattle in the field, upon the horses, upon the asses, upon the camels, upon the oxen, and upon the sheep, a very grievous plague. And Jehovah shall separate between the cattle of Israel and the cattle of Egypt. And there shall nothing die of all that belongs to the sons of Israel."

(Exodus 9:1-4, MKJV)

Note that Israel and all their agriculture and economy would be saved, if they kept the feasts, and worship God above all else. These were the conditions for divine protection. We all know of the Ten Plaques that ravished and destroyed the Egyptian economy, agriculture, and eventually, the firstborn.

Halfway on their journey, they came to Mount Sinai and were given a total body of Law for their new country. But because they ignored the Ten Commandments right from the start, the sacrificial system was added as a schoolmaster, to keep them in line.

After giving most of the Law of Moses, as well as other Commandments, Precepts, and Judgments to the Israelites, they were promised blessings if they obey, and alternately given warnings of the results if they would disobey God's Word.

Notice the following description:

> "Jehovah shall strike you with **lung disease** and with a **fever**, and with an **inflammation**, and with an extreme **burning**, and with the **sword**, and with **blasting**, and with **mildew**. And they shall pursue you until you perish."

(Deuteronomy 28:22, MKJV)[Emphasis mine]

The translation needs to be carefully considered, word by word.

Be aware that due to the way God's creation works, diseases will come, if they ignore God's instructions. The Bible shows that Jehovah created the current animal kingdoms and humankind, and created it to balance the species and make it sustainable for thousands of years. However, for us humans to stay healthy, directions were given as to how to manage the ecological system and our food supply. If these laws are violated, the Bible shows that viruses will spread and end up in humans.

Let's look at every description.

~~~~~

Lung disease

The scripture describes an initial lung disease. These diseases will pursue Israel until they begin to die. Several waves of these pandemics may come. One leads to the rest. Time and again, people's immune systems will weaken until they finally succumb to the damage done to their bodies.

~~~~~

Mildew

Since they were living in tents, coughing when sick can add moisture to the fabric, and in a hot climate, the disease can exist in the moisture on the fabric for a while. Mildew can set in, and make their temporary dwellings infectious.

~~~~~

Burning

The skin can become dry, and the inflammation can heat the body, with the dry skin appearing white at first,
~~~~~

then blue. It turns white like Mildew due to lack of blood flow, as the body adjusts to protect internal organs, such as the lungs. It will be as if people feel their skin burn.

~~~~~

Blasting

Blasting refers to how the skin feels having been blasted by a hot wind for many hours. The burning sensation from extreme infection is the same.

~~~~~

Sword

If Israel becomes sick and weak, enemies can easily attack them. The enemies may come after them with the sword. During the Exodus, many nations felt threatened by a few million Israelites moving north past their cities to their Promised Land and would attack if their spies report that the Israelites were sick and diseased. However, a reference to the sword could also indicate that many will die, either directly of the virus or indirectly of the consequences.

This was the warning to Israel. But it is clearly also a warning to the world. In the New Testament era, God also reaches out to humanity as a whole, through Jesus Christ and true Christianity. The Creator knew His creation and wanted people to be healthy and productive.

God loves us and has told us how to protect ourselves, our families, and our nations. Don't see it as a vengeful God who is deliberately punishing us with these curses.

However, the warnings were in the Bible. So let's look at the bigger section of this narrative in the Bible.

There is a section in the book of Deuteronomy that is generally called the blessings and curses chapter. The reader will do good to read the whole chapter. In this eBook, we will look at the curses, as you may make the connection from what is seen on the news every day:

"And it shall be, if you will not listen to the voice of Jehovah your God, to observe and to do all His commandments and His statutes which I command you today, all these curses shall come on you and overtake you. You shall be cursed in the city, and cursed in the field. Your basket and your store shall be cursed. The fruit of your body shall be cursed, and the fruit of your land, the increase of your cows, and the flocks of your sheep. You shall be cursed when you come in, and cursed when you go out. Jehovah shall send on you cursing, vexation, and rebuke, in all that you set your hand to do, until you are destroyed, and until you perish quickly, because of the wickedness of your doings by which you have forsaken Me. Jehovah shall make the plague cling to you until He has consumed you from off the land where you go to possess it. Jehovah shall strike you with **lung disease and with a fever, and with an inflammation, and with an extreme burning, and with the sword, and with blasting, and with mildew**. And they shall pursue you until you perish. And your heavens over your head shall be bronze, and the earth that is under you iron. Jehovah shall make the rain of your land powder and dust. It shall come down from the heavens on you until you are destroyed.

(Deuteronomy 28:15-25, MKJV)[Emphasis mine]

Doesn't it sound like Corona-virus pandemics? And lockdowns? Cursed when we go in, cursed when we go out? Cursed in the cities being locked in?

The prophets repeatedly warned Israel about the consequences of not following God's laws concerning farming, food supply, cleanliness, and human behavior.

At the inauguration of the Temple in Jerusalem, King Solomon prayed and asked God to hear their prayers if the plaques and pandemics ravished the population.

"If there is famine in the land, if there is plague, blasting, mildew, locusts; if there are stripping locusts; if their enemy encircles them in the land of their cities, whatever plague, whatever sickness, any prayer, any supplication from any man of all Your people Israel, who shall each know the plague of his own heart, and shall spread forth his hands toward this house, then hear in Heaven Your dwelling-place, and forgive, and do, and give to every man according to all his ways, whose heart You know. For You, You only, know the hearts of all the sons of Adam."

(1 Kings 8:37-39, MKJV)

Before this section in scripture on the blessings and curses in Deuteronomy 28, there are plenty of laws given about hygiene, food, meat, disposing of waste, city development, separation of people, quarantine, and looking after the poor and hungry.

The consensus in the world is that we are not under the Old Testament law, and hence we can ignore all of it. The truth is not so simple. In the next chapter, this question needs to be discussed. Some of the laws have been valid for many thousands of years, and are still in force. The causes of the Corona-virus pandemics are in the Old Testament section. There is a reason why the Bible contains the Old Testament section, and we need to look at it. There is valuable information.

The animal creation and the way it functions have stayed the same. Ever since the Creation Week, the ecological systems are still exactly the same. The crucifixion has not changed that. Cause and effect are still in force today. Animal designs have not changed. Pigs still roll in the filth. Lions still tear animals apart. So maybe we should look at how Israel would be saved from pandemics.

Only in the future, in the seventh millennium, after Christ's return, we were promised that animal metabolism would change. Notice a future prophecy concerning a new heaven, a new earth, and a New Jerusalem:

> "The wolf and the lamb will feed together, and the lion will eat straw like the ox; and dust will be the food of the snake. They will not hurt nor destroy in all My holy mountain, says Jehovah."
>
> (Isaiah 65:25, MKJV)

The Bible shows that only then will animal biochemistry change. But it did not change during the Crucifixion. Hence the Noahide dietary laws still apply today.

Biblical principles on farming, food supply, diet, health, and design of cities are still applicable today.

We will now carry on in the next chapters to describe the practical solutions and the reason for the pandemics in the world. Humanity can mostly prevent these disasters if only we can believe the Bible and follow God's instructions.

As a historical book, the Bible has been proven to be correct time and again, thanks to archeological discoveries. As a prophetic book, the Bible has been proven to be true through many fulfilled prophecies.

As a scientific book, the Bible has also been proven to be correct if we rectify some translation issues, and understand what the prophets of old meant.

https://www.christianpost.com/voices/scientific-facts-in-the-bible.html

https://www.youtube.com/watch?v=t2sMJMXDiH4

2 Which Law?

If we understand that the Bible is true, then there is still the issue of what applies to us today.

~~~~~

The Ten Commandments

There are many arguments for the Ten Commandments being still valid and required of us today. It is God's law of love. If we love God, and our neighbour, we will fulfil the Ten Commandments. We will shortly deal with it in a few verses.

"And behold, one came and said to Him, Good Master, what good thing shall I do that I may have eternal life? And He said to him, Why do you call Me good? There is none good but one, that is, God. But if you want to enter into life, keep the commandments. He said to Him, Which? Jesus said, You shall not murder, you shall not commit adultery, you shall not steal, you shall not bear false witness, honor your father and mother, and, you shall love your neighbor as yourself."

(Matthew 19:16-19, MKJV)

There is a clear distinction between the Ten Commandments and the Law of Moses. Notice the events at Mount Sinai:
~~~~~

"And it happened when Moses had made an end of writing the words of this Law in a book, until they were finished, Moses commanded the Levites who carried the Ark of the covenant of Jehovah, saying, Take this book of the Law, and put it in the side of the Ark of the covenant of Jehovah your God, so that it may be there for a witness against you."

(Deuteronomy 31:24-26, MKJV)

The Ten Commandments were written on tablets of stone, and placed inside the Ark. The sacrificial Law was included in the Law of Moses, which was added due to their sin, and was placed in the side of the Ark, as a witness against Israel. The Law of the sacrificial system was against the people, not the Ten Commandments. The Ten Commandments were thundered by God from above Mount Sinai and define love. Transgressions thereof define sin.

The sacrificial system was added as a witness against Israel's sin and was in force in Jerusalem for all who wants forgiveness and redemption. But now the sacrificial system was replaced by the sacrifice of Jesus Christ at His crucifixion, and we act on it by faith and not by Law, repenting and maintaining the Commandments of God.

There is a lot to be said in defence of the Ten Commandments, but that alone will not save us from disease epidemics. However, it is a good start.

Consider the role of the Commandment against adultery and fornication.

"Whoever commits adultery with a woman lacks understanding; he who does it destroys his own soul."

(Proverbs 6:23, MKJV)

And what has science so far discovered concerning diseases that spread because of fornication and adultery?

The most serious is HIV/AIDS. This disease weakens the immune system, and allows the bodily infiltration and spread of other diseases, such as Corona-viruses. Understand that this weakens the population and makes humanity susceptible to the spread of Corona-viruses.

~~~~~

The Noahide Laws

The Noahide laws were evident from the life of Noah, and since the world consists of Noah's children, we should all give them serious consideration. The Jewish Talmud describes them, but the exact interpretation is somewhat uncertain and controversial. We will only look at Biblical instructions and proof.

Some of them are included in the Ten Commandments. There is for instance a further demand for a proper setup of court systems to fairly judge offenders. The first law is against idolatry or idol worship. But the seventh law deals with meat suitable for human consumption.

When many uncircumcised gentiles enter the new Christian Church in the first century, the issue of circumcision and adherence to the Law of Moses became a burning issue. In the Jerusalem conference, the issue was resolved as the apostles delved into the Old Testament scriptures and other evidence.

It was concluded that uncircumcised Christians from other countries have no need for circumcision, and therefore is not obliged to maintain the Law of Moses.
~~~~~

However, adherence to the Noahide laws was still required, and obviously also the Ten Commandments.

Notice the discussion in the book about the Acts of the Apostles:

"Therefore my judgment is that we do not trouble those who have turned to God from among the nations, but that we write to them that they should abstain from pollutions of idols, and from fornication, and from things strangled, and from blood."

(Acts 15:19-20, MKJV)

This was described in a letter sent to the Churches in Asia and beyond.

"For it seemed good to the Holy Spirit and to us to lay on you no greater burden than these necessary things: that you abstain from meats offered to idols, and from blood, and from things strangled, and from fornication; from which, if you keep yourselves, you shall do well. Be prospered."

(Acts 15:28-29, MKJV)

This was a summary, and it was suggested by the Apostels that these were taught in the synagogues in Israel, Asia and elsewhere in the Roman Empire, and possibly as far as Ethiopia in Africa, hence the reference that these are taught by Moses everywhere.

We will deal with the laws concerning meat suitable for human consumption.

Never eat any animal found dead. If it was not alive and well, don't eat it! If the cause of death is unknown, don't eat it!

Scavengers and other meat-eating animals seek out the weak and diseased animals to hunt. They are easier to catch and kill. Therefor never eat an animal killed by lions and other such hunters.

We should never eat blood. We should never drink blood, particularly warm blood directly from an animal. In Asia and Africa, the habit of some nomad tribes is the piercing of a vain of a camel or cattle and drinking the warm blood. This way, diseases enter the human species, and Corona-viruses can jump to humans and spread.

When clean animals such as sheep and cattle are killed for consumption, the blood must be immediately and completely drained. On farms and abattoirs, clean animals can be mercifully receive a blow to the head for immediate death, and the blood immediately drained. Jewish Kosher or Islam Halaal methods are correct. But some atheistic nations and governments don't follow these laws. This is a concern for the spread of Corona-viruses.

Noah gathered two pairs of unclean animals and seven pairs of clean animals for survival in the Ark. Noah and his family knew about God's viewpoint on what animals are suitable for human consumption. Obviously, they only consumed clean animals while in the Ark, as well as afterward, while they restarted their farming industry.

Therefore it is clear that the law on clean and unclean meat existed long before the Law of Moses, and is valid for the current creation of animals. It is, therefore, valid for humankind today. It is valid for you and me. It is valid for all cities and countries. Violation creates an environment where Corona-viruses can breed and spread.

Clean and unclean meat

The list of clean animals is mentioned in the Old Testament scriptures. Obviously, then there was no need to repeat them in the New Testament section. It is in your Bible.

The general idea is only to eat animals that eat plants exclusively in their natural habitat. Avoid animals that eat other animals. Avoid animals that wallow in the dirt. Their bodies contain enzymes and viruses that can consume other meat, including humans!

Leviticus 11 describes in detail which animals are clean and unclean. We will look at some verses in more detail.

"And Jehovah spoke to Moses and to Aaron, saying to them, Speak to the sons of Israel, saying, these are the animals which you shall eat among all the animals that are in the earth. Whatever divides the hoof, and is cloven-footed, chewing the cud, among the animals, that you shall eat."

(Leviticus 11:1-3, MKJV)

Animals that chew the cud eat plants and are clean. They need to continue chewing grass to dissolve plant material, and they need to eat a lot to get enough nourishment, so they eat all day long. Cattle, sheep, and goats are clean animals, and can be consumed by humans.

In rare circumstances, cattle can carry diseases, but it is often caused by unbiblical farming methods, such as mixing products from unclean animals into their feed. One example is Mad Cow disease, which originate from pigs. Other problems are the habit of injecting cattle with female hormones to fatten them so that a higher price is obtained at the abattoir. If cattle were allowed to roam free and live off grass, it would be a safe source of meat.

"Only, you shall not eat these of them that chew the cud, or of them that divide the hoof: the camel, for he chews the cud but does not divide the hoof; he is unclean to you."

(Leviticus 11:4, MKJV)

In the Middle East countries and also North Africa, the habit of drinking blood from camels may cause diseases.

https://www.who.int/news-room/fact-sheets/detail/middle-east-respiratory-syndrome-corona-virus-(mers-cov)

One of the Corona-virus pandemics originated from the Camels of the Middle East. It was labeled the MERS virus, or MERS-COV pandemic. MERS obviously stands for Middle Eastern Respiratory Disease.

"And the rock badger, because he chews the cud, but does not divide the hoof; he is unclean to you."

(Leviticus 11:5, MKJV)

https://en.wikipedia.org/wiki/Badger_culling_in_the_United_Kingdom

Bovine Tuberculosis originated from Badgers, and can be deadly for humans.

"And the hare, because he chews the cud but does not divide the hoof; he is unclean to you."

(Leviticus 11:6, MKJV)

A hare may have Tularemia. It is caused by the bacterium Francisella tularensis virus. It is a zoonotic disease and can cause infection in humans with serious consequences.

"And the swine, though he divides the hoof and is cloven-footed, yet he does not chew the cud; he is unclean to you. You shall not eat of their flesh, and you shall not touch their dead body. They are unclean to you."

(Leviticus 11:7-8, MKJV)

Swine can cause many diseases in humans, including ringworm, erysipelas, leptospirosis, streptococcosis, campylobacterosis, salmonellosis, cryptosporidiosis, giardiasis, balantidiasis, influenza and infection with pathogenic E. coli.

The swine farming industry has caused Mad Cow disease on people and cattle farms. England recently had to kill cattle worth a billion Pounds to curtail the spread. It also is a factor in the spread of diseases.

https://en.wikipedia.org/wiki/Environmental_impact_of_pig_farming

"These you shall eat of all that are in the waters: whatever has fins and scales in the waters, in the seas, and in the rivers, them you shall eat."

(Leviticus 11:9, MKJV)

"And all that have not fins and scales in the seas, and in the rivers, of all that move in the waters, and of any living thing that is in the waters, they shall be an abomination to you. They shall even be an abomination to you. You shall not eat of their flesh, but you shall have their carcasses in abomination."

(Leviticus 11:10-11, MKJV)

Some sea creatures don't have scales and fins, like barracuda and shark. They eat other sea flesh, and are unclean.

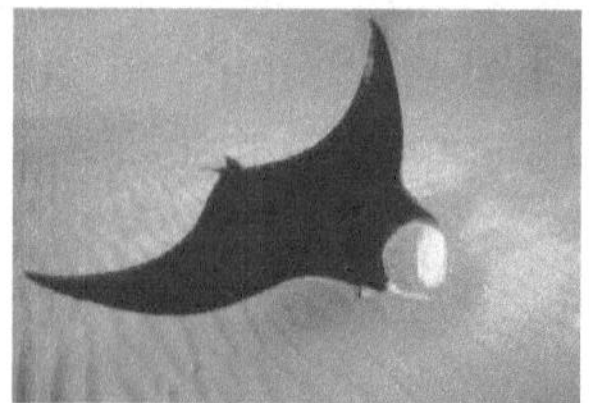

Some live from the dead meat that sinks to the bottom of rivers and oceans. Eating the scavengers of the sea can be deadly, particularly during a red tide. It leads to diseases, and the opportunity for viruses and deadly bacteria to spread to humans.

"And you shall have these in abomination among the fowls. They shall not be eaten, they are an abomination: the eagle, and the black vulture, and the bearded vulture, and the kite, and the falcon, according to its kind; every raven according to its kind; and the little owl, and the cormorant, and the eared owl; and the barn owl, and the pelican, and the owl-vulture; and the stork, the heron according to its kind, and the hoopoe, and the bat. Every flying swarming creature going on all four, it is an abomination to you."

(Leviticus 11:16-20, MKJV)

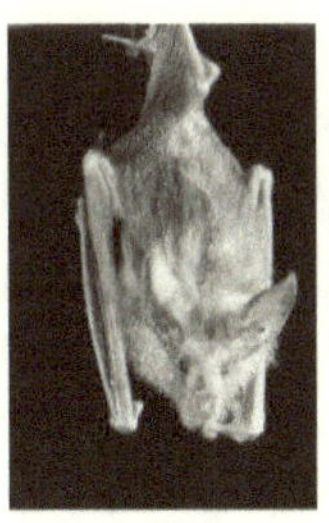

Bats can carry rabies and viruses related to SARS, and may be the original hosts of nasty viruses such as Ebola and Nipah, which causes deadly brain fevers in people.

"Yet you may eat these of any flying swarming thing that goes on all four, those which have legs above their feet, to leap with on the earth. You may eat these of them: the locust after its kind, and the bald locust after its kind, and the long horned locust after its kind, and the short horned grasshopper after its kind."

(Leviticus 11:21-22, MKJV)

Therefore John the Baptist was authorized to live from locusts while he was preaching in the desert. It is a clean animal, living only from eating plants.

"But every other flying swarming thing which has four feet shall be an abomination to you. And you shall be unclean for these. Whoever touches their dead body shall be unclean until the evening. And whoever carries the carcass of them shall wash his clothes and be unclean until the evening; even every living thing which divides the hoof, and is not cloven-footed, nor chews the cud, they are unclean to you. Everyone that touches them shall be unclean. And whatever goes on its paws, among all the living things that go on all four, those are unclean to you. Whoever touches their dead body shall be unclean until the evening. And he that carries their dead bodies shall wash his clothes and be unclean until the evening. They are unclean to you."

(Leviticus 11:23-28, MKJV)

We would be in a much better position concerning the health of the world if Biblical principles were followed by every nation.

"These also shall be unclean to you among the swarming things that swarm on the earth: the weasel, and the mouse, and the great lizard after its kind;"

(Leviticus 11:29, MKJV)

There are disease concerns with wild and pet rats and mice. They can carry many diseases including hantavirus, leptospirosis, lymphocytic choriomeningitis (LCMV), Tularemia and Salmonella.

Sometimes children keep mice as pets, but they could invite diseases into their home, endangering the lives of their parents. They brought the bubonic plague to Europe that killed millions.

"and the gecko, and the monitor, and the lizard, and the sand lizard, and chameleon."

(Leviticus 11:30, MKJV)

Lizards and reptiles carry a range of germs including bacteria, viruses, parasites and worms. Many of these can be transmitted on to the family of reptile owners, such as Salmonella, Botulism, leptospirosis, trichinellosis , and campylobacteriosis. Some cause cancer in people.

We must isolate ourselves and our families from these. Most particularly, they should never be eaten at all!

"These are unclean to you among all that swarm. Whoever touches them when they are dead shall be unclean until the evening. And whatever shall fall on any of them when they are dead, shall be unclean, whether any vessel of wood, or clothing, or skin, or sack; whatever vessel in which work is done, it must be put into water, and it shall be unclean to the evening. So it shall be cleaned. And every earthen vessel in which any of them falls, whatever is in it shall be unclean. And you shall break it. Of all food which may be eaten, that on which such water comes shall be unclean. And all drink that may be drunk in every such vessel shall be unclean. And every thing on which any part of their dead body falls shall be unclean; whether it is the oven, or ranges for pots, they shall be broken down. They are unclean, and shall be unclean to you. But a fountain or pit, with a collection of water, shall be clean. But that which touches their dead body shall be unclean. And if any of their dead body falls on any sowing seed which is to be sown, it shall be clean. But if any water is put on the seed, and any part of the dead body falls on it, it shall be unclean to you. And if any animal among those you may eat dies, he that touches its dead body shall be unclean until the evening. And he that eats of its dead body shall wash his clothes and be unclean until the evening. He also that carries its body shall wash his clothes and be unclean until the evening. And every swarming thing that swarms on the earth shall be an abomination. It shall not be eaten. Anything going on its belly, and any going on all four, and all having many feet, even every swarming thing that swarms on the earth, you shall not eat them. For they are an abomination. You shall not defile yourselves with any swarming thing that swarms, neither shall you make yourselves unclean with them, so that you should be defiled by them. For I am Jehovah your God, and you shall sanctify yourselves, and you shall be holy, for I am holy. Neither shall you defile yourselves with any kind of swarming thing that swarms on the earth. For I am Jehovah who brought you up out of the land of Egypt, to be your God. You shall therefore be holy, for I am holy. This is the law of the animals, and of the fowl, and of every living creature that moves in the waters, and of every creature that swarms on the earth, to make a difference between the unclean and the clean, and between the creature that may be eaten and the creature that may not be eaten."

(Leviticus 11:31-47, MKJV)

We should avoid the unclean animals and isolate them from our homes, farming practices and workplaces.

https://en.wikipedia.org/wiki/Kosher_foods

We should consider the Kosher and Halaal requirements. In the long run it is good for humanity, and will prevent the breeding and spread of Corona-viruses, which eventually harm nations.

See the link below to some viral information. Most of them come from unclean animals, and can spread to humans through the wet meat market food chain, but also through fleas, ticks and mosquitos. Even in farming these unclean animals should be absent.

https://viralzone.expasy.org/678

Current worldwide pandemics are linked to wildlife trade, mostly practiced by atheist nations.

https://www.nationalgeographic.com/science/2020/01/new-corona-virus-spreading-between-humans-how-it-started/

Interbreeding forbidden

We are forbidden to experiment with species, to change God's creation from His original design.

> "You shall keep My statutes. You shall not let your cattle breed with different kinds. You shall not sow your field with two kinds of seed. And you shall not allow clothing mixed of linen and wool to come on you."

(Leviticus 19:19, MKJV)

We cannot know and experiment with the outcome. It may lead to disastrous consequences, and weaken future species, leading to susceptibility to disease. This may lead to the breeding and altering of viruses that may then easily infect the current species.

Mixed linen fibres can weaken the cloth. It can also lead to excessive wear and tear, as well as static building up and causing discomfort to people to the extent that rashes can form. This weakens the skin, making it susceptible to infection by viruses.

In the long term, the people of the land and its animals become defiled.

> "And the land is defiled. Therefore I visit its wickedness on it, and the land itself vomits out those who live in it. You shall therefore keep My statutes and My judgments, and shall not commit any of these abominations, neither the native, nor any stranger that lives among you."

(Leviticus 18:25-26, MKJV)

These ordinances were for everyone, Jew and Gentile. Experimentation by scientists, particularly in atheistic nations, may spawn disease epidemics, even Corona-viruses.

The Bible does allow the strengthening of existing species. That is what Jacob did with his flock.

"And Jacob separated the lambs, and set the faces of the flocks toward the striped, and all the black in the flock of Laban. And he put his own flocks by themselves, and did not put them with the flock of Laban. And it happened when the stronger flocks conceived, Jacob laid the rods before the eyes of the flocks in the troughs, so that they might conceive among the rods. But when the flocks were feeble, he did not put them in. And usually it came to be, the weak ones were Laban's and the stronger ones Jacob's."

(Genesis 30:40-42, MKJV)

The natural microevolution that God designed into the genetics came into play. But gross scientific experiments to circumvent God's creation and natural order will lead to problems and diseases.

"Only be sure that you do not eat the blood. For the blood is the life. And you may not eat the life with the flesh. You shall not eat it. You shall pour it on the earth like water. You shall not eat it, so that it may go well with you and with your sons after you, when you shall do what is right in the sight of Jehovah."

(Deuteronomy 12:23-25, MKJV)

The blood of unclean animals has to be avoided at all cost. The human body may not survive from infections that come from it. However, some labs deliberately acquire blood from unclean animals such as bats to do tests. Perhaps they should have left the bats alone?

Most of the Corona-viruses of the past few decades originated from unclean animals, such as bats, pangolins, cats, wild dogs, and pigs.

https://coronavirusexplained.ukri.org/en/article/und0007/

https://www.ncbi.nlm.nih.gov/pmc/articles/PMC3676139/table/T1/?report=objectonly

In the next chapter we will see how Biblical principles should have been used to protect the nations.

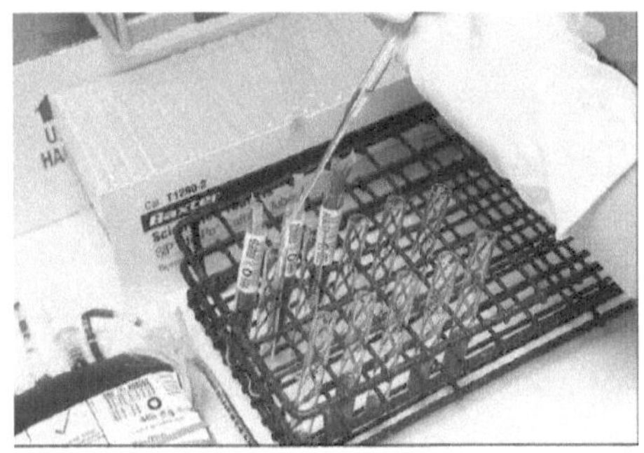

3 Waste products

The way we get rid of waste products can also be a reason for the spread of Corona-viruses.

During the Exodus, Moses instructed the Israelites, considering hygiene. One aspect was how to deal with human waste products discretely and safely. The people were to leave the camp, dig a hole in the bush, relieve themselves, and cover it up with sand. This is important.

It has to be eliminated immediately; else, disease may spread. Some animals are drawn to it and can ingest the viruses. Those animals were created as the rubbish processors of the animal kingdom. Their bodies can handle our filth. However, our bodies cannot overcome their filth!

Notice the clear instruction in the Bible:

"You shall also have a place outside the camp where you shall go forth. And you shall have a paddle on your weapon. And it shall be, when you sit down outside, you shall dig with it, and shall turn back and cover that which comes from you."

(Deuteronomy 23:12-13, MKJV)

Moses continued to describe that as a leader sanctioned by God, he didn't want to find any exposed human waste. It would be ungodly to allow it to lie around, for God's people to step on it. This may spread diseases in the community.

During the time of the Dark Middle Ages, cities used open urinals and open tunnels under them that would carry the waste products away. Eventually, rats and fleas that lived off this caused the disease to spread that killed an estimated 200,000,000 people. Two hundred million, only in Europe! It was called the Black Plague. Some called it the Bubonic plague, although in the science community, some dispute that. However, it does not matter. The main issue was the open pits and urinals with open sewer tunnels, and rats that roam in the night between ships in the harbour and the filth of the city. This eventually turned out to be deadly. It is a clear violation of Biblical principles concerning the disposal of human waste products.

Closed sewer systems in modern cities are correct. However, some cities may still have such open systems. Biblical hygiene prohibits such practices. They are a source of the spread of Corona-viruses.

In some high-rise buildings in modern cities, these sewage pipes can also be a source of disease. What if there is a leak? A sick person higher up in the building can infect others lower down if there is a leak or breakage in the pipe. These practices are a corona-virus disaster waiting to happen if not well maintained. Such is life in cities. People are, in fact, in danger of diseases, if buildings and city infrastructure are not well maintained, and people stay on top of each other.

Hygiene and cleanliness

After the sin of Israel at Mount Sinai during the Exodus, Moses instituted the sacrificial system to be a schoolmaster to keep the nation on the straight and narrow path of righteousness.

This was utilized until Jesus died at the hands of misguided and sinful humankind and leaders. The crucifixion shocked all of Jerusalem into the futility of humankind to do self-rule in righteousness. It showed us our sinfulness.

"For the Law which has a shadow of good things to come, not the very image of the things, appearing year by year with the same **sacrifices**, which they offer continually, they are never able to perfect those drawing near."

(Hebrews 10:1, MKJV)[Emphasis mine]

The implementation of the sacrificial system could have caused diseases such as Corona-viruses to flourish. Having warm animal flesh sacrificed on the Altar continually was a health risk to the priests and High Priest. The various clean animals would be carved open near the fire of the Altar. Various animals, such as bulls, sheep, goats, and doves, were routinely sacrificed.

Hence quite a rigorous washing routine and quarantine were also implemented. Notice how clean the whole process was performed. Without continual washing viruses could breed and spread.

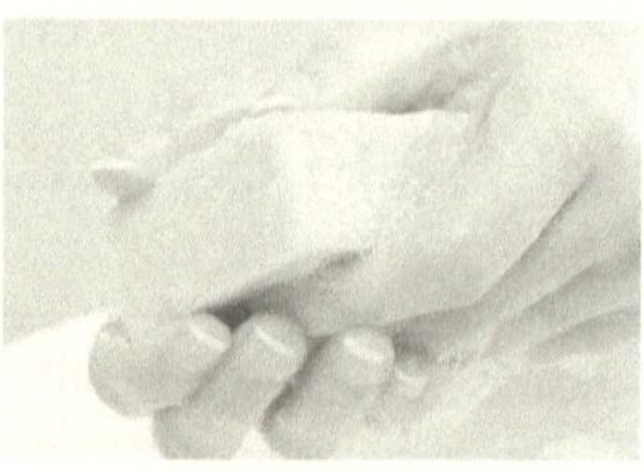

Let's look at the cleanliness of the sacrificial system, and also the need to burn the leftovers to prevent health problems:

"And the sons of Aaron the priest shall put fire on the Altar and lay the wood in order on the fire. And the priests, Aaron's sons, shall arrange the parts with the head and the fat on the wood that is on the fire on the Altar. But its inward parts and its legs he shall wash in water. And the priest shall burn all on the Altar, a burnt sacrifice, an offering made by fire, of a sweet savor to Jehovah."

(Leviticus 1:7-9, MKJV)

Roasted meat of a clean animal may be eaten the next day. However, any leftovers were burned on the third day.

"But the rest of the flesh of the sacrifice on the third day shall be burned with fire."

(Leviticus 7:17, MKJV)

This prevented bacteria such as Listeria from growing and killing people. Some meat factories claim to have processes that prevent this, but even in modern times, there were outbreaks, and many people became sick, and some have died. The main reason is that they also process unclean animal meat, in particular pork.

The best rule by the Book is to roast clean meat and eat it the same day. The cold at night may render it safe to eat more of it the next day. By the third day, it must be burnt outside the camp. So only prepare as much as would be used up in two days, or give the rest away to the poor. This is good advice from the Bible, particularly in warm climates.

Abattoirs need to operate under very clean conditions. Meat processing plants should not process any unclean animals. Hot and wet meat markets where a mixture of live and dead clean and unclean animals is very dangerous. It breeds diseases. Modern fast travel and international trade will also ensure quick worldwide spread, and hence pandemics.

Having a concentration of pig carcases lying in hot conditions, beginning to dissolve in a warm meat open market is a breeding ground for viruses and disease. Avoid these at all cost.

~~~~~

Quarantine

When Israel started their Exodus from their slavery in Egypt, they had skin problems. The poor diet as slaves, together with the stress, left them with skin diseases. Places on their bodies where they were whipped have not healed. They struggled with skin diseases and were susceptible to leprosy. This had to be contained; else, it would spread to others.
~~~~~

Moses correctly implemented quarantine procedures. These are the same when there are pandemics caused by Corona-viruses.

Let's see how they handled the problem of contagious diseases during the Exodus.

Firstly the person is isolated and observed carefully. A determination needs to be made as to the exact medical problem.

"And Jehovah spoke to Moses and Aaron, saying, When a man has a rising in the skin of his flesh, or a scab or bright spot, and it is in the skin of his flesh like the plague of leprosy, then he shall be brought to Aaron the priest, or to one of his sons the priests. And the priest shall look on the plague in the skin of the flesh. And if the hair in the plague has turned white, and the plague in sight is deeper than the skin of his flesh, it is a plague of leprosy. And the priest shall look on him and shall pronounce him unclean. And if the bright spot is white in the skin of his flesh, and in sight is not deeper than the skin, and the hair of it has not turned white, then the priest shall shut up the plague seven days."

(Leviticus 31:1-4, MKJV)

If the person is diagnosed as serious, then quarantine procedures were implemented, first for a week, and if not healed, then for another week, or more.

"And the priest shall look on him the seventh day. And behold, if the plague in his sight is stayed; the plague has not spread in the skin, then the priest shall shut him up seven days more."

(Leviticus 13:5, MKJV)

The diseased person had to stay in his tent for a week, and if not healed, for more weeks.

If the person heals, then the person and all clothes, and even the bedding, must be washed before the person can leave the quarantine.

"And in the seventh day the priest shall look on the scab. And behold, if the scab has not spread in the skin, nor is in sight deeper than the skin, then the priest shall pronounce him clean. And he shall wash his clothes and be clean."

(Leviticus 13:34, MKJV)

If it can't be sure whether an affected garment is clean and sanitized, then it must be burnt or incinerated. Some thick wool garments may seem clean on the surface, but deep inside the fibres the virus or bacteria may still linger.

"And he shall burn that garment, whether warp or woof, in wool or in linen, or anything of skin in which the plague is. For it is a fretting leprosy. It shall be burned in the fire."

(Leviticus 13:52, MKJV)

Tents were set up outside the camp to house those that had to be quarantined. The priest would go out to inspect and determine the diagnoses. If a person was healed, then a thanksgiving offer would be made to God, and the person would be allowed back into the camp. At first, the healed person would stay out of his tent in the camp for another week. Only then can the person join his or her family. Every step of the way, the person and clothes must be washed. This was a careful procedure to ensure the epidemic is not allowed to spread.

"And the priest shall go forth out of the camp. And the priest shall look, and behold, if the plague of leprosy is healed in the leper, then the priest shall command to take two clean live birds for him that is to be cleansed, and cedar wood, and scarlet, and hyssop. And the priest shall command that one of the birds be killed in an earthen vessel over running water. He shall take the living bird, and the cedar wood and the scarlet and the hyssop, and shall dip them and the living bird in the blood of the slain bird, over the running water. And he shall sprinkle on him that is to be cleansed from the leprosy seven times, and shall pronounce him clean, and shall let the living bird loose into the open field. And he that is to be cleansed shall wash his clothes, and shave off all his hair, and wash himself in water so that he may be clean. And after that he shall come into the camp, and shall stay outside his tent seven days. But on the seventh day he shall shave all his hair off his head and his beard and his eye-brows; even all his hair shall he shave off. And he shall wash his clothes. He also shall wash his flesh in water, and he shall be clean."

(Leviticus 14:3-9, MKJV)

They only way to get a Corona-virus outbreak under control is to follow these procedures carefully, perhaps even forcefully.

It is clear from the Bible that quarantine procedures are required and must be maintained. This way, we can protect our families from disease and loss of life!

Today we have hospitals that do quarantine procedures for us, but they are expensive. Hospitals are rather geared towards operations and such medical procedures. Nations and cities should rather have other buildings that only deal with quarantine procedure and feeding patients a healthy diet so that hospitals are not burdened with pandemic patients, and neglect other health problems.

~~~~~

Concrete Jungle

One of the reasons for the rapid spread of Corona-viruses is the modern practice of building towers as in the days of Babel. It is not good to have people live one on top of another.

Long ago, humankind also got the idea of bringing people together in a large city with a high-rise building. This way, people could be more productive and be under the control of the king day and night. The synergy of working together in one big building would advance science, technology, and arms development. However, it would also allow disease and plaques to spread rapidly among the population.

After the Flood, the families of Noah spread and multiplied. The main focus was on agricultural production.

But Nimrod had other plans.

"And Cush fathered Nimrod. He began to be a mighty
one in the earth. He was a mighty hunter before
Jehovah. Therefore it is said, Even as Nimrod the
mighty hunter before Jehovah. And the beginning of his
~~~~~

kingdom was Babel, and Erech, and Accad, and Calneh, in the land of Shinar."

(Genesis 10:8-10, MKJV)

Nimrod would build the tower of Babel, but God put an end to that.

"And Jehovah came down to see the city and the tower which the sons of Adam had built. And Jehovah said, Behold! The people is one and they all have one language. And this they begin to do. And now nothing which they have imagined to do will be restrained from them. Come, let Us go down and there confuse their language, so that they cannot understand one another's speech. So Jehovah scattered them abroad from that place upon the face of all the earth. And they quit building the city. Therefore the name of it is called Babel; because Jehovah confused the language of all the earth there. And from there Jehovah scattered them abroad on the face of all the earth."

(Genesis 11:5-9, MKJV)

The Biblical way for humanity is to rather spread out over the earth. We should be close to the farming community, which is a better way of life. People should understand where their food comes from. Then there is a short process from a live healthy animal to meat on the table. But with massive cities, there is a long process, which could be an opportunity for diseases to spread. Notice the warning from the prophet:

"Woe to those who join house to house, laying field to field, until the end of space, and you are made to dwell alone in the middle of the land! Jehovah of Hosts swore in my ears, Truly many houses shall be deserted, big and fair, without inhabitant."

(Isaiah 5:8-9, MKJV)

The building of huge skyscrapers in cities for people, till a farmer is alone in a huge industrialised farm, was not God's idea. It will contribute to health problems in the cities. Some ancient cities became sick, and the inhabitants deserted them

These high-rise towers in the current concrete jungles are an ideal place for Corona-viruses to spread. Add the huge amount of fast transport across the world in jet planes, and the world is prepped for repeated pandemics.

Archaeological discoveries have suggested that some cities in ancient times became infected, and some of

its inhabitants died. Those that survived eventually burned the city and fled to other places.

~~~~~

Borders

Good borders promote peace. The Biblical narrative suggests good borders with controlled movement.

"And the Philistines were beaten, and they did not come anymore into the border of Israel. And the hand of Jehovah was against the Philistines all the days of Samuel. And the cities which the Philistines had taken from Israel were given back to Israel, from Ekron even to Gath. And Israel delivered its borders out of the hand of the Philistines. And there was peace between Israel and the Amorites."

(1 Samuel 7:13-14, MKJV)

Good borders promote peace, safety, and protection from pandemics. In countries where people enjoy freedoms, they may be vulnerable to evil Godless nations that will see them as vulnerable doves, to misuse their generosity. Without border control, the free people will not be safe, and the country will descend into crime, necessitating a police state. Such is also the case when border control does not stop the spread of Corona-viruses.

"You have set all the borders of the earth; You have made summer and winter. Remember this, the enemy has cursed, O Jehovah, and the foolish people have blasphemed Your name. Do not deliver the soul of Your
~~~~~

turtle dove to the multitude; forget not the congregation of Your poor forever."

(Psalms 74:17-19, MKJV)

In the modern world, such moves to strengthen the border controls are seen as racist. But God has warned the nations that this will eventually erode their freedoms, and they will eventually live under strict police control to prevent the decimation of the population. Such is the case today.

The saying of old is that good fences make good neighbours.

In a parable about God sending His Son to claim His inheritance, it is clear that a good fence is needed to protect the fruits of hard labor. Notice the parable, and again the clear requirement of a good fence.

"And He began to speak to them by parables. A man planted a vineyard, and **set a fence about it**, and dug a wine-vat, and built a tower, and he let it out to vinedressers, and went away."

(Mark 12:1, MKJV)[Emphasis mine]

It is clear that the fence in this parable was the borders of Israel, and Jesus was sent to harvest the souls of the saints, at first in Israel, but later from the whole world.

"Therefore, still having one son, his own beloved, he also sent him to them last of all, saying, they will respect my son. But those vinedressers said among themselves, This is the heir! Come, let us kill him and the inheritance shall be ours. And they took him and killed him and cast him out of the vineyard."

(Mark 12:6-8, MKJV)

And so Jesus Christ was crucified.

The point is that it is Biblical to make fences, to have borders, and to control the flow of goods and people, to prevent the spread of diseases, and in particular Corona-viruses.

Strict border controls should prevent the spread of Corona-viruses. This is essential, since lately these viruses have been spreading on an increasing rate, and if not stopped, will become the norm and decimate cities and economies.

~~~~~

International Travel

In the Last Days, humanity will learn how to travel far and wide.
~~~~~

"But you, O Daniel, shut up the words and seal the book, even to the time of the end. Many shall run to and fro, and knowledge shall be increased."

(Daniel 12:4, M KJV)

Knowledge will increase to do good, but also evil such as developing chemical and bio weapons. International travel will also grow and expand. In the Last Days, thousands of infected people can travel across the continents and seas in a day, and infect many thousands more the very next day.

Sanitation and disinfection against Corona-viruses was lacking at airports. And a week or two in quarantine at the destinations would be unthinkable for the travellers. However, considering the continual outbreaks of pandemics in some countries, is this not necessary?

International Trade

How important is rapid and free international trade? Is it more important than the health of nations? Recently several nations have ratified open and free international trade treaties. That obviously has opened the world to the spread of pandemics.

Open, unrestricted, unlawful and uncontrolled trade can bring pandemics.

"By the host of your iniquities, by the iniquity of your trade, you have profaned your holy places; so I brought a fire from your midst; it shall devour you, and I will give you for ashes on the earth, before the eyes of all who see you."

(Ezekiel 28:18, MKJV)

The biological violence is also spread to nations, as some ignore regulations through corrupt means. Border officials sometimes are bought by unscrupulous traders to ignore laws. And so pandemics can lead to economic collapse, and it can lead to violence in the midst of cities.

Preventing Hunger

It is essential not to let people go hungry. The Biblical principle is to allow at least the whole population to eat well. Notice the instruction in your Bible to Israel.

"And when you reap the harvest of your land, you shall not wholly reap the corner of your field. And you shall not gather the gleaning of your harvest. And you shall not glean your vineyard. And you shall not gather the leavings of your vineyard. You shall leave them for the poor and the stranger. I am Jehovah your God."

(Leviticus 19:9-10, MKJV)

During the Sabbaths, with worshippers traveling to Jerusalem for the Festivals, there would be ample food for the travellers.

"And you shall proclaim on the same day that it may be a holy convocation to you. You shall do no work of labor. It shall be a statute forever in all your dwellings throughout your generations. And when you reap the harvest of your land, you shall not completely reap the corner of your field. When you reap the gleaning of your harvest, you shall not gather. You shall leave them to the poor and to the stranger. I am Jehovah your God."

(Leviticus 23:22, MKJV)

When people go hungry and begin to starve, their immune systems get weak, and they are susceptible to disease. It becomes a problem when they are traveling as well. This becomes the danger to the cities and the spread of diseases such as the Corona-viruses. Therefore God insists that the travellers must not go hungry but eat well. Jerusalem had to be protected from the spread of diseases, else people will flee Jerusalem, and it will depopulate. Hence when Jesus and His disciples walked to a place of worship on the Sabbath, they were permitted to glean food from the corners of farms.

"At that time Jesus went through the grain fields on the sabbath day. And His disciples were hungry, and began to pluck the heads of grain and to eat."

(Matthew 12:1, MKJV)

This prevented hunger and therefore assisted in preventing vulnerable worshippers from entering the congregations and contracting diseases.

Many ancient pagan and gentile cities in the world did not practice this, and people's immune systems became vulnerable. This way, epidemics spread, and eventually, citizens fled their disease-ridden cities. Many have so been abandoned.

~~~~~

Experimentation in Laboratories

In some labs in the world, scientists are experimenting with viruses and diseases. Unclean animals are experimented with in various unholy ways. These days DNA reengineering is done to test the results. This is dangerous. Humankind is meddling in the Creation of God. We can never completely fathom the wisdom of God. Some things are better left alone.

Due to the theory of Evolution, the assumption may be that we have the same kind of flesh, since we all
~~~~~

apparently evolved from the same cell. But the Bible indicates differently.

> "Not all flesh is the same. Humans have one kind of flesh, animals in general have another, birds have another, and fish have still another."

(1 Corinthians 15:39, ISV)

Viruses, enzymes, and bacteria of one animal type should not end up in another type.

For instance, scavengers and animals that wallow in the filth have enzymes that consume flesh. Swine has enzymes that consume human flesh. Some people have suffered greatly because of this. Some people have had to have some of their flesh cut away in hospitals to save their lives. Some have died.

But in some labs, scientists are playing god. Accidents will happen, and viruses will leak out, and spread worldwide. Obviously these scientists believe in the Theory of Evolution, have not read a Bible let alone believe in the Creator, and are experimenting with God's Creation. As scientists "advance" their experimentation into forbidden areas, we may see more devastating viruses come out and spread worldwide.

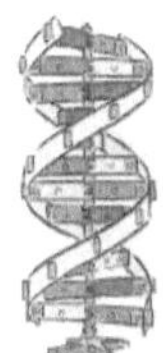

4 Judgment by God?

Are the Corona-virus outbreaks and pandemics a judgment by God? Let's consider that question from the pages of your Bible.

Some people don't want to believe in God, for they question why a loving God can allow these disasters to happen to humanity.

We need to answer this enigma.

After repeated catastrophic events caused Job to lose his family, he had many arguments with God. He also asked how it is that God could allow these disasters.

But humanity does not study to know God. Humanity has turned its back on God. It believes Darwin, who was a rookie concerning science. Darwin observed microevolution, not macroevolution, and humankind in their eagerness to avoid God's rule, commandments, guidance, and instructions, continued to expand the concept into macroevolution. They believed in a creation without a Creator. More is discussed in the 3rd edition of the eBook "Harmonizing the Creation Week and Science".

By now, the reader must understand that God has given us a lot of instructions that would have prevented Corona-viruses from breeding and spreading worldwide.

And so, just like Job, humanity feels that they can't fathom God.

"The Almighty, whom we cannot find out, is exalted in power; and to judgment and overflowing righteousness He does no violence."

(Job 37:23, MKJV)

In the end, we will have to admit that God is right. He is not violating His righteousness if He allows the spread of Corona-virus pandemics. We have been warned!

In a future prophecy, the world is judged because it does not worship and acknowledge the Creator.

"saying with a great voice, Fear God and give glory to Him! For the hour of His judgment has come. And worship Him who made the heaven and the earth, and the sea, and the fountains of waters."

(Revelation 14:7, MKJV)

What is meant by judgment?

When a bridge is built, the judgment of the designers and workers come when heavy vehicles move over it, and heavy storms batter it.

When a ship sails the heavy seas, a judgment of the engineers and builders come when freak waves test it for strength.

Once a city infrastructure is built, big storms bring judgment on it to see if it can cope with wind and floods.

In the Last Days, judgment will come to test the occupants of big cities. And so Corona-viruses test humanity to know if they followed Biblical instructions. If not, we cannot blame God. Nations and peoples that argued against the existence of God, our Creator, are judged. Disobedience of our Creator left us vulnerable.

We have followed in the path of Babel, building massive towers again. We have followed Babylon and brought this upon ourselves.

"And another angel followed, saying, The great city,
Babylon, has fallen, has fallen; because of the wine of
the anger of her fornication; she has made all nations to
drink."

(Revelation 14:8, MKJV)

This prophecy may apply to a specific city according to
some, but it applies to all cities in the world that traded
with her and fashioned itself after the examples and ways
of Babylon.

So how can we blame God?

Fifty years ago, the Bible was read in some
governments. Prayer was heard in Parliaments. Leaders
knew of God's instructions. To some extent, they fashioned
societies accordingly.

But then the prayers stopped. Bibles were removed.
The daily sacrifice of prayers to the God of Abraham,
Isaac, and Jacob, the Father of Jesus Christ, was banned!

Pictures and statues of the two tablets of stone with
the Ten Commandments on were banned!

Notice the following prophecy concerning the Last
Days, or the end of days. There may be different
interpretations, but notice the big issue of the daily sacrifice
being taken away:

"And He said, Go, Daniel! For the words are closed up
and sealed until the end-time. Many shall be purified,
and made white, and tried. But the wicked shall do
wickedly. And none of the wicked shall understand, but
the wise shall understand. And from the time that
the **daily sacrifice** shall be taken away, and the
desolating abomination set up, a thousand two hundred

and ninety days shall occur. Blessed is he who waits and comes to the thousand three hundred and thirty-five days. But you go on to the end, for you shall rest and stand in your lot at the end of the days."

(Daniel 12:9-13, MKJV)[Emphasis mine]

And prayers are a daily sacrifice.

"Let my prayer be set forth before You as incense, and the lifting up of my hands as the evening sacrifice."

(Psalms 141:2, MKJV)

And now Christianity is also banned from schools. And the youth is losing direction.

The Corona-virus pandemics are a judgment on the wrong way of living.

So we cannot blame God! He has warned the nations. It is in their Bibles. We can, however, take a look at practical advice and guidance given us by the Creator, and change direction in our economies, infrastructure, farming methods, food supply, and our cities.

~~~~~

The Aftermath

Does our Bible tell us about the aftermath when the continual Corona-virus pandemics come? How can nations prepare for and manage the dangerous situation that we enter into?
~~~~~

The Apostle Paul warned us about the times we live in. We can see the reality of this in the light of the pandemics. Let's comment on each verse:

"Know this also, that in the last days grievous times will be at hand."

The free and easy life will be over, putting pressure on society and its infrastructure.

"For men will be self-lovers, money-lovers, boasters, proud, blasphemers, disobedient to parents, unthankful, unholy,"

Society, in general, doesn't appreciate how good they have had it in recent times. Growing demand for more and more has spawned discontent, fuelled by rebellious music, and violent Hollywood movies. Different ideologies bring clashes of ideas, and gullible young people have been funded to have protest movements, resulting in violence and damage to property. The Corona-virus pandemics will demonstrate this in a most vivid way. Main Stream Media will greedily absorb this for sensationalism. Celebs will misuse this to bolster their social media profiles with excitement to gain an ever-growing following, all in the name of ratings and obviously sponsorship and money.

Where are the days when pious parents went with their children to church, united in the depression, willing to live on a penny a day with government aid and rebuild their societies?

"without natural affection, unyielding, false accusers, without self-control, savage, despisers of good,"

On both sides, Main Stream Media and Social Media, the accusations fly, and people get worked up by false news. Some savagely take to the streets to loot shops and even homes from good people that have worked a lifetime to accumulate a little. The riots get out of control, and the goodwill that has been carefully built up can vanish in a month.

"traitors, reckless, puffed up, lovers of pleasure rather than lovers of God,"

Instead of visiting their local places of worship, people visit their entertainment centers, their restaurants and pubs, disco's and night clubs. This way, Corona-viruses are spread easily. Dancing people exhale the virus in masses, and with their immune systems weakened by alcohol, they all catch the diseases. The added prevalence of narcotics means people totally abandon all common sense and create the most fertile breeding ground for disease epidemics.

Where are the days when families rather went to church to learn sobriety and self-control?

In churches people behave and are under control. They sit down and listen to God's Word. They can avoid singing and loudly exhaling the virus, and keep a distance from each other. On the other hand, revellers at these entertainment places easily lose self-control, and the viruses will spread fast.

And entertainment in some places lead to harlotry as well, which can be another sure way of spreading viruses.

"For of these are those who creep into houses and lead captive silly women loaded with sins, led away with different kinds of lusts,"

(2 Timothy 3:1-6, MKJV)

We surely are in the age where the Apostle Paul's description of the problem is true.

Therefore society must rethink its ways. If the hospitals are full, and death is at our doors, will people turn to God, so that we can win against the viruses?

Jesus gave us a general outlay of the Last Days. We can highlight some of it as the aftermath of the coming of the Corona-viruses.

These pandemics will bring animosities between nations. The liberal idea of allowing different religions from different countries to come with an ever-growing amount of migrants and refugees could lead to animosities. Leaders and governments will fall, as they did not recognize how these various religions can offend each other. Understand that atheism is also a religion, and so also is Darwinism driven to a firm belief of macroevolution. These religions don't really mix. The leadership will find that out the hard way.

When people begin to die, hospitals overflow, and governments make bad decisions that cause economic hardship and hunger. The fault lines will show. Even Christians will have difficult times in countries that used to be Christian a hundred years ago. Are we paying the price for leaders who tried to force Christian pastors to perform gay marriages, which is clearly against God's Will?

Notice the section of prophecy by Jesus Christ:

"For nation will rise against nation, and kingdom against kingdom. And there will be famines and pestilences and earthquakes in different places. All these are the beginning of sorrows. Then they will deliver you up to be afflicted and will kill you. And you will be hated of all nations for My name's sake. And then many will be offended, and will betray one another, and will hate one another. And many false prophets will rise and deceive many. And because iniquity shall abound, the love of many will become cold. But he who endures to the end, the same shall be kept safe. And this gospel of the kingdom shall be proclaimed in all the world as a witness to all nations. And then the end shall come."

(Matthew 24:7-14, MKJV)

Governments will have problems, as different ethnic and religious groups may not really accept the authority of the other. When strict laws and measures come to try and control the outbreak, these groups may rebel and cause havoc. Some will be worked up by social media, and others will be worked up by mainstream news media, as governments and even tycoons in the industries think that now is the time to promote their ideologies. They think now is the time to do social reengineering. This is just fuel to the fire.

Christians were told to accept the authority of the country they are in. So they will cooperate with strict rules to curtail Corona-virus outbreaks, as long as they can be allowed in some way to continue with their worship services,

"So that the one resisting the authority resists the ordinance of God; and the ones who resist will receive judgment to themselves. For the rulers are not a terror to good works, but to the bad. And do you desire to be not afraid of the authority? Do the good, and you shall have praise from it. For it is a servant of God to you for good. For if you practice evil, be afraid, for it does not bear the sword in vain; for it is a servant of God, a revenger for wrath on him who does evil. Therefore you must be subject, not only for wrath, but also for conscience' sake. For because of this you also pay taxes. For they are God's servants, always giving attention to this very thing."

(Romans 13:2-6, MKJV)

However, other groups may not be happy with strict health measures. They may feel oppressed as minorities and then will stand up against the police. Riots will ensue, and in the turmoil, the Corona-viruses will even spread more. It might have been easier if different nations and religious groups were in their own countries. They would more readily accept strict laws from leaders and authorities, consisting of their own ethnic groups and religions. However, they may rebel if it comes from other ethnic rulers of other religions.

The Corona-viruses may show up the fault lines and may hasten the coming of the Last Days described in the Bible.

What can we do now?

Since humankind have not been following Biblical principles, and have believed the Theory of Macro Evolution, and hence stopped believing in the Creator, we are now in the day and age where the growing influence of the Godless may cause regular Corona-virus pandemics.

How can we protect ourselves and our families in the face of this growing threat?

It would have been fantastic to have the living Jesus Christ and His resurrected Apostles with us today to heal the Christians instantly.

"And as you go, proclaim, saying, The kingdom of Heaven is at hand. Heal the sick, cleanse the lepers, raise the dead, cast out demons. You have received freely, freely give."

(Matthew 10:7-8, MKJV)

However, there is a lot we can do today in terms of real worship and prayer. Be aware that there is also a responsibility from our side. We can't expect the miraculous healing of unconverted atheists.

"For the heart of this people was fattened, and they have heard with their ears dully; and they closed their eyes; lest at any time they should see with their eyes, and hear with their ears, and understand with their heart, and should be converted, and I should heal them."

(Acts 28:27, MKJV)

We are expected to study our Bibles and believe in God and His Son, Jesus Christ. We must open our eyes to the Bible and see the evil in our society. We should hear when Christian preachers work to teach us the ways of Jesus Christ. Keep the Commandments and strive to understand and be converted. These are essential requirements.

Furthermore, pray for wisdom. Pray that we will become aware of the dangers to our health. The Spirit of God will help us like a "sixth sense" to avoid pitfalls. Seek truth and understanding and practice hygiene.

Also, follow a healthy diet.

In the book of Daniel, we are treated to the need for daily intake of vegetables and fruit.

"But Daniel laid on his heart that he would not defile himself with the king's food, nor with the wine which he drank. So he asked permission of the chief of the eunuchs that he might not defile himself."

(Daniel 1:8, MKJV)

Eating rich pastries and consuming alcohol every day leads to a weak immune system. The pastries already lead to some inflammation, which the body must fight to contain. Alcohol further weakens the immune system. And with the socializing that gets out of hand with much drunkenness, we enter the ideal situation where we can fall prey to Corona-viruses.

Daniel asked instead to consume vegetables and drink plenty of water. After ten days, the difference was clear!

"I beg you, try your servants ten days. And let them give us vegetables to eat and water to drink. Then let our appearance be seen before you, and the appearance of the boys who eat of the king's food. And as you see, deal with your servants. So he listened to them in this matter, and tried them for ten days. And at the end of ten days their faces looked fairer and fatter in flesh than all the boys who had eaten the king's food."

(Daniel 1:12-15, MKJV)

Follow a good diet with clean meat vegetables and salads every day. It should be priority in our lives. Make sure we budget for it. Rather put aside purchases of luxury and fancy clothes, and the new car. Make sure we can eat a good meal of vegetables with some lean clean meat every day. Also eat it with love in a peaceful home environment, as emotions affect our digestive system.

"Better is a dinner of vegetables where love is, than a stalled ox and hatred with it."

(Proverbs 15:17, MKJV)

Also eat fresh fruit for fillers in-between meals. Avoid the processed junk some industries want you to eat and drink, with its sugars and carbonated fizzle.

God brought Israel into a good land with plenty fruit, but the leaders polluted the land and the people with junk, just as in recent times in modern cities.

"And I brought you into a plentiful country, to eat its fruit and its goodness; but when you entered, you defiled My land and made My inheritance an abomination."

(Jeremiah 2:7-8, MKJV)

Make sure our bodies are given the best chance to survive a virus attack!

Submit to authorities

We need to submit to authorities in these days of the pandemics.

"Let every soul be subject to the higher authorities. For there is no authority but of God; the authorities that exist are ordained by God. So that the one resisting the authority resists the ordinance of God; and the ones who resist will receive judgment to themselves."

(Romans 13:1-2, MKJV)

It is for our own good. Consider the need for others to protect themselves and their families.

~~~~~

Exercise

The Apostle Paul was mostly concerned with exercising our faith towards Godliness. However, physical exercise is also required in today's world where people sit at a desk, sit in the car, and sit at home, having devices that do most of the work.

"But refuse profane and old-womanish tales, and exercise yourself to Godliness. For bodily exercise profits a little, but Godliness is profitable to all things,
~~~~~

having promise of the present life, and of that which is to come."

(1 Timothy 4:7, MKJV)

Physical exercise is important in today's world with all its transport mechanisms that rob us of enough daily exercise.

Being fattened and overweight can be detrimental to our health. Be sure to get exercise to maintain an optimal body. Also, do breathing exercises. Needless to say, smoking is a health risk. There is, in fact, no evidence that any Biblical character ever smoked. Getting drunk was also prohibited. Only in a few cases, this happened by accident.

"And do not be drunk with wine, in which is excess, but be filled with the Spirit,"

(Ephesians 5:18, MKJV)

Avoid contact with any fluid of others, even airborne spray.

In severe pandemics, wear a mask when going outside into public places.

Increase indoor air. Some old buildings may have damp walls. There may be mould taking hold in cracks. Make sure walls are clean and sealed. Else the rooms must be disinfected regularly. If a sick person is in the house and coughs, droplets can gather in cracks and on surfaces. In such cases the home needs to be cleaned regularly.

https://www.webmd.com/lung/mold-mildew

Finally, save all the cash for weeks or months of having to isolate and quarantine. Prepare for economic hardship.

~~~~~

Seek medical advice

Some in the faith may have heard a radical idea that Christians are not to seek medical advice.

The Apostle Timothy had a stomach ailment. But instead of just praying for him, the Apostle Paul also told him to take medicine.

"Drink water no longer, but use a little wine for your stomach's sake, and for your frequent infirmities."

(1 Timothy5:23, MKJV)

Wine at that time was readily available and used as medicine. It is clear that Christians should be ready to use good medicine in a responsible manner.
~~~~~

One of the main four Gospel writers and one of the 12 Apostles was a medical doctor and certainly continued with his practice when visiting the churches and brethren. Hence he was loved for his assistance, which he would often do for free, for the poor.

"Luke, the beloved physician, and Demas, greet you."

(Colossians 4:14, MKJV)

Luke was not prevented from practicing as a medical doctor. Hence Paul pertinent mentions him in his greetings as the "beloved physician." Don't refuse any medical assistance. If the preventative measures did not protect the family and sickness comes, contact the doctor or hospital. Your bible advises you to do so.

~~~~~

If we are old

`Older people become vulnerable to flu and virus pandemics. Special care should be taken to eat well and get exercise. Walk daily. A brisk walk of a kilometre or mile can help.
~~~~~

Special lung exercises are required to keep the lungs in good conditions.

https://www.healthline.com/health/how-to-increase-lung-capacity

Iron supplements can also help the blood to carry oxygen to the rest of the body. But consult with your doctor. Consider the side effects.

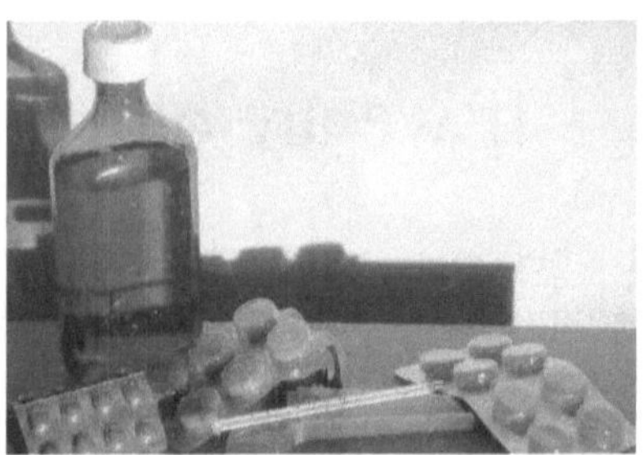

If we do contract a respiratory disease like Corona-virus, and the hospitals are full, and we suffer breathing, be sure to have extra oxygen available in the form of a pressurized bottle. Another appliance that can help is a CPAP system.

https://en.wikipedia.org/wiki/Positive_airway_pressure

These are small devices, and many families can afford these. Just be sure that you do not share masks. The masks of such appliances will obviously become infected with the first person to use a new mask. So the mask should be the exclusive property of one patient. Alternately it can be disinfected for a day with special disinfectant solutions. Else it will be a sure way to spread the Corona-virus!

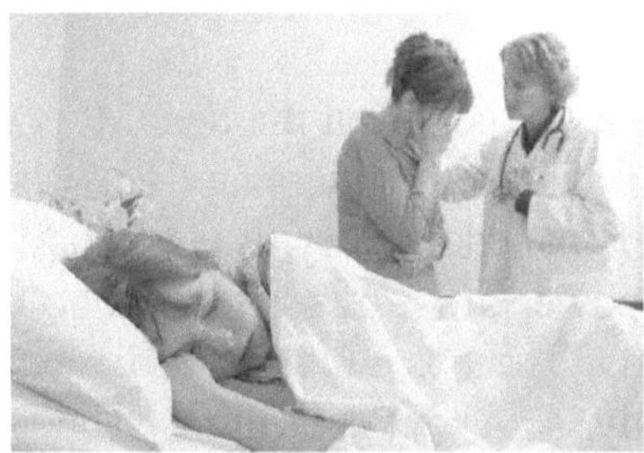

If we are too weak to survive, or if we have loved ones that succumb to the pandemic, remember there is hope beyond the grave. The Creator promised resurrection to all. Hence the next section is fitting in these desperate times.

Life after death

If humanity does not turn to God and study their Bibles, reintroduce Christian studies in schools for all pupils, and prayers in parliament, what will our future look like? While the immediate future may look bleak, and death is stalking us, there is hope in the afterlife. There is the hope of a resurrection for all.

"So also the resurrection of the dead. It is sown in corruption, it is raised in incorruption; it is sown in dishonor, it is raised in glory; it is sown in weakness, it is raised in power; it is sown a natural body, it is raised a spiritual body. There is a natural body, and there is a spiritual body. And so it is written, "The first man, Adam, became a living soul," the last Adam was a life-giving Spirit. But not the spiritual first, but the natural; afterward the spiritual. The first man was out of earth, earthy; the second Man was the Lord from Heaven. Such the earthy man, such also the earthy ones. And such the heavenly Man, such also the heavenly ones. And according as we bore the image of the earthy man, we shall also bear the image of the heavenly Man. And I say this, brothers, that flesh and blood cannot inherit the kingdom of God, nor does corruption inherit incorruption. Behold, I speak a mystery to you; we shall not all fall asleep, but we shall all be changed; in a moment, in a glance of an eye, at the last trumpet. For a trumpet shall sound, and the dead shall be raised incorruptible, and we shall all be changed. For this corruptible must put on incorruption, and this mortal must put on immortality. But when this corruptible shall put on incorruption, and when this mortal shall put on immortality, then will take place the word that is written, "Death is swallowed up in victory. O death, where is your sting? O grave, where is your victory?" The sting of death is sin, and the strength of sin is the Law. But thanks be to God who gives us the victory through our Lord Jesus Christ."

(1 Corinthians 15:42-57, MKJV)

The exact detail of the resurrections is understandable from your Bible. To understand more about your future in Christ, an eBook about "Life after Death" is available.

It is an expansive subject that requires another book. Be sure that if our loved ones or we succumb to disease or pandemics, it is not the end. In Jesus Christ, our story continues.

5 Future Prophecies

On the Mount of Olive, Jesus gave His disciples a view of a future worldwide scenario in the Last Days. It started with a prophecy that the Temple will be destroyed, which did happen 40 years later, in 70 AD, according to the Sign of Jonah. For more on this, see the eBook on The Sign of Jonah – expanded.

The prophecy extended from their time during the year of the Crucifixion to the fall of Jerusalem and them fleeing to Petra, the rock city in the mountains south of Jerusalem. But now, over two thousand years later, will the same situation play out again, perhaps on a worldwide scale?

Let's consider each verse:

"And as He sat on the Mount of Olives, the disciples came to Him privately, saying, Tell us, when shall these things be? And what shall be the sign of Your coming, and of the end of the world?"

(Matthew 24:3, MKJV)

There are two questions here. This first question is about the destruction of the physical Temple. The second question is about the situation before the return of Messiah.

"And Jesus answered and said to them, Take heed that no man deceive you. For many will come in My name, saying, I am Christ, and will deceive many."

Matthew 24:4-5, MKJV)

Jesus expected that many leaders will come into the Faith, and then later walk out and draw a following, changing doctrines and loosing Truth. There would be many Christian churches, of which some are closer, and others further away from the original Faith.

"And you will hear of wars and rumors of wars. See that you are not troubled, for all these things must occur; but the end is not yet. For nation will rise against nation, and kingdom against kingdom. And there will be famines and **pestilences** and earthquakes in different places. All these are the beginning of sorrows."

(Matthew 24:6-8, MKJV)[Emphasis mine]

More and more nations will be confronted by disease and pandemics. Problems in the food chain coupled with rapid international travel can lead to pestilences, epidemics and pandemics to spread. And this may cause more confrontation, isolation and public uprisings.

"Then they will deliver you up to be afflicted and will kill you. And you will be hated of all nations for My name's sake. And then many will be offended, and will betray one another, and will hate one another. And many false prophets will rise and deceive many. And because iniquity shall abound, the love of many will become cold. But he who endures to the end, the same shall be kept safe."

(Matthew 24:9-13, MKJV)

The love and tolerance between religious groups, ethnic groups, and races may wane. And if crime is not punished, but overlooked by authorities, civil wars may ensue.

In the dangers, many will hopefully turn to God, and churches, to seek divine intervention and protection.

"And this gospel of the kingdom shall be proclaimed in all the world as a witness to all nations. And then the end shall come."

(Matthew 24:14, MKJV)

The next few verses then was aimed at the Apostles and their immediate danger when first the Temple would be destroyed, and then Jerusalem raided, and Israel as a whole collapsed.

Eventually it talks of the time just before the return of Messiah:

"And immediately after the tribulation of those days, the sun shall be darkened and the moon shall not give her light, and the stars shall fall from the heaven, and the powers of the heavens shall be shaken."

(Matthew 24:29, MKJV)

From the Biblical point of view tribulation may come as a consequence of the Corona-viruses caused by unclean food, unbiblical farming methods, and the mishandling of the food chain. The civil unrest, burning of properties, and possible civil war, may cause smoke to darken the sky in places.

The reference to pestilence is what is important to this study.

Consequences of Corona-viruses

As soldiers huddled close in trenches during WWI, a flu epidemic broke out. There are several factors that caused that pandemic.

As the world took sides, and allegiances were honoured, soldiers from other areas of the globe came together to fight each other. Their bodies have not yet developed immunity to viruses in their new environments. Soldiers were also forced into the battle. A mild flu wasn't an excuse to stay home. Furthermore, the hardships of war caused people to begin to eat any unclean animal they can lay hands on. It was a recipe for a pandemic. Thus war caused the pandemic, and later affected it.

Israel began their Exodus, and moved through other countries and lands to their Promised Land. They had all the factors that could cause a pandemic. People were overworked in Egypt as slaves and some were weak. They travelled through other countries for which their bodies had not yet developed immunity. They went hungry and the danger existed that they could begin to eat dead and unclean animals along the way. Corona-viruses could jump to humans and mutate. Also the surrounding nations were scared of them and would attack if they perceived that the Israelites were weakened by an epidemic. The danger would still exist even when they arrive in their Promised Land.

That is why Moses the prophet urged them to obey all the rules and laws given to them, and combined these factors in his prophecy to them, warning them of the consequences of disobedience.

"Jehovah shall strike you with lung disease and with a fever, and with an inflammation, and with an extreme burning, and with the sword, and with blasting, and with mildew. And they shall pursue you until you perish."

(Deuteronomy 28:22, MKJV)

The generals of WWI did not consider these warnings, and hence the pandemic came in 1918 during the war. More soldiers died of the pandemic than of actual war.

https://en.wikipedia.org/wiki/Spanish_flu

Eventually the generals realised that the war had to end, or they risk decimating their armies and economy back home. They, and their politicians, gathered to hammer out some peace treaties. They blamed the war on Germany, and expected war reparations. No mercy was granted. Sanctions were further imposed. It caused economic collapse and hyperinflation in Germany. The German people had to stand up against Europe. They chose a war leader, and fought back, and started WWII.

After WWII ended, the UN was formed. The USA also started an air bridge and helped Germany to restart their economy. It was a more humane and Christian thing to do. So far WWIII have been avoided.

The link between pandemics and war must not be forgotten.

This is the danger, and why these prophecies were given.

~~~~~

Economic collapse

Corona-virus pandemics may hasten the tribulations of the Last Days. Governments and ethnic groups may want to protect their countries, religions and cities. And so another prophecy may be fulfilled later.

"And I saw another beast coming up out of the earth. And it had two horns like a lamb, and he spoke like a dragon. And it exercises all the authority of the first beast before him, and causes the earth and those dwelling in it to worship the first beast, whose deadly wound was healed. And it does great wonders, so that it makes fire come down from the heaven onto the earth in the sight of men. And it deceives those dwelling on the earth, because of the miracles which were given to it to do before the beast, saying to those dwelling on the earth that they should make an image to the beast who had the wound by a sword and lived. And there was given to it to give a spirit to the image of the beast, so that the image of the beast might both speak, and might cause as many as would not worship the image of the beast to be killed. And it causes all, both small and great, rich and poor, free and bond, to receive a mark on their right hand, or in their foreheads, even that not any might buy or sell except those having the mark, or the name of the beast, or the number of its name."

(Revelation 13:11-17, MKJV)
~~~~~

In the coming cashless world, those that may oppose the new world order may have their accounts frozen, and isolated from world economy. This will have a further negative effect on economic activity and trade. Every political action has an economic reaction, some quite negative and unexpected.

This may cause unresolved conflicts from WWII to flare up, as the economic impact of the Corona-viruses is wreaking havoc on the world economies.

~~~~~

Leftovers of WWII

There are unresolved issues around the world after WWII ended. Thanks to economic prosperity, and a voice in the UN, most have not flared up. However, a catalyst like Corona-virus pandemics and economic may bring those to the forefront, and there are many of these issues.

https://en.wikipedia.org/wiki/Aftermath_of_World_War_II

This may bring us back to the situation of wars and rumours of wars becoming prevalent.

"And when you shall hear of wars and rumors of wars, do not be troubled. For it must happen, but the end shall not be yet."
(Mark 13:7, MKJV)
~~~~~

Religious differences

The push for a world government and a new world order by some may not possible in the current situation. It has a big hurdle due to religious differences. Different countries have allowed migrant workers and refugees to enter the workforce, without much regard to religious differences and requirements. If the world and its entire population were of the same religion, then it can face a pandemic and economic collapse together. But with different belief systems it could be a problem.

For instance, the Christian faith believes that Jesus Christ is the head in all religious matters. Jesus was the greatest Prophet.

But then, most of the Jews do not believe in Jesus as the Christ, but believes in the God of Abraham, Isaac and Jacob.

Then there is Islam, who believes in Allah, the God of Abraham and Ismael, and Mohammed as their prophet. Jesus to them was a normal earthly prophet that was born about two thousand years ago. The Quran suggests that He is not the Son of God, did not pre-existed before that, and is not alive in Heaven today.

These are fundamental differences. Apart from these, there are the Hindu and Buddhist religion, and others.

Whereas Christians may evangelise, radical Islam wants to dominate with minarets blaring the call to prayers over other communities, leading to animosity among other believers.

When the Corona-viruses strike and the economic collapse begin, fault lines may appear, and tribulation comes.

~~~~~

Hastening the Last Days

From the Talmud the understanding comes that humanity has six millenniums to do as they please, till Messiah comes to herald the seventh millennial rule of Christ. The Second Advent will happen supernaturally. Jewish tradition suggests that we are now in the year 5780 since Adam. Therefor there are still 220 years before the return of Jesus Christ.

But according to the Bible, that may not be the case. There is an indication that God may send His Son earlier to save the world.

"And unless those days should be shortened, no flesh would be saved. But for the elect's sake, those days shall be shortened."

(Matthew 24:22, MKJV)

This prophecy happened 40 years after the crucifixion. So it was true for the saints in Jerusalem.
~~~~~

However, over two thousand years later, Jews are dispersed over the western world, and so are also the other tribes of the lost House of Israel as well. Christians are also dispersed to many countries. So this is also true for the next 220 years.

The situation may deteriorate since humanity in general is not following Biblical principles. Corona-viruses pandemics will increase, in particular since humanity is not following principles in terms of farming practices, food processing and scientific experimentation. This will make things worse; hence Messiah will come in less than 220 years. We can only hope, pray and look forward to that glad day with anticipation, when Jesus will lead the world in following Godly principles, and there will be no more Corona-viruses.

"And I, John, saw the holy city, New Jerusalem, coming down from God out of Heaven, prepared as a bride adorned for her Husband. And I heard a great voice out of Heaven saying, Behold, the tabernacle of God is with men, and He will dwell with them, and they will be His people, and God Himself will be with them and be their God. And God will wipe away all tears from their eyes. And there will be no more death, nor mourning, nor crying out, nor will there be any more pain; for the first things passed away."

(Revelation 21:2-4, MKJV)

May God speed that day. The world sorely needs Messiah to return.

From Psalms 103 we read the following:

"Bless Jehovah, O my soul, and forget not all His benefits; who forgives all your iniquities; who heals all your diseases; who redeems your life from ruin; who crowns you with loving-kindness and tender mercies; who satisfies your mouth with good; your youth is renewed like the eagle's. Jehovah works righteousness and judgment for all who are pressed down. He made known His ways to Moses, His acts to the sons of Israel. Jehovah is merciful and gracious, slow to anger, and rich in mercy."

(Psalms 103:2-8, MKJV)

The ways of God concerning health was made known to Moses.

When Christ returns, nations will learn from Him. He will correctly teach the nations concerning many things, including the health laws.

"For, behold, I create new heavens and a new earth. And the things before will not be remembered, nor come to mind. But be glad and rejoice forever in that which I create; for behold, I create Jerusalem a rejoicing, and her people a joy. I will rejoice in Jerusalem, and I will rejoice in My people; and the voice of weeping will no more be heard in her, nor the voice of crying be heard in her. There will not be an infant, nor an old man that has not filled his days. For the child will die a hundred years old; but the sinner who is a hundred years old will be despised. And they will build houses and live in them; and they will plant vineyards and eat their fruit. They will not build, and another live in them; they will not plant, and another eat. For like the days of a tree are the days of My people, and My elect will long enjoy the work of their hands. They will not labor in vain, nor bring forth for terror. For they are the seed of the beloved of Jehovah, and their offspring with them. And it will be, before they call I will answer; and while they are still speaking, I will hear. The wolf and the lamb will feed together, and the lion will eat straw like the ox; and dust will be the food of the snake. They will not hurt nor destroy in all My holy mountain, says Jehovah."

(Isaiah 65:17-25, MKJV)

One day this will be fulfilled. We can all look forward to the resurrection. We will one day see our loved ones again, and good days of freedom ahead, free of Corona-viruses. After Messiah comes, eventually the world will have much better days, and the resurrected saints will see the utopia eventually, the way God intended it in paradise, as he made it for Adam and Eve.